Dan L. Allbeta

LAOS

TRAVEL GUIDE

2023 - 2024

plus 53 Common Expressions and Phrases to Sound like a Local

PLUS! COMPLIMENTARY TRAVEL JOURNAL, CHECKLIST & ITINERARY

Laos

Travel Guide
2023 - 2024

*Your Indispensable Travel Compass and Companion to Explore and Enjoy **LAOS** like never before!*

Travel Tips, Tricks & Techniques

Dan L. Allbeta

Table of Content

PREFACE

I'm happy you took a bold step by investing in this one of a kind travel guide (companion and compass). I hope it will be more than a travel guide and perhaps be a dependable travel companion throughout your stay.

Welcome to Laos, a special place in Southeast Asia where time slows down, and the mix of culture and nature unfolds. In this guide, you're going to explore a country with ancient traditions, beautiful landscapes, and friendly people.

Laos, also known as the "Land of a Million Elephants," is rich in history and different landscapes. From the busy streets of Vientiane, the calm capital, to the beauty of the Mekong River, every part of this country has a unique story to tell, and you get to be part of it.

This place is waiting to reveal its awesomeness to you.

Let the adventure begin!

Dan L. Allbeta

"Laos is a canvas painted with the brushstrokes of simplicity, where every stroke tells a story of contentment."

- Paul Theroux

Take a Glance

Picture a place where time moves at its own pace, revealing a uniqueness woven with ancient traditions, breathtaking landscapes, and the warm embrace of Laotian hospitality.

Land of a Million Elephants

Laos, often called the "Land of a Million Elephants," shows its beauty with a rich history and different geography.

- *From the lively streets of Vientiane*, the laid-back capital, to the calm banks of the Mekong River, every corner tells stories of a unique culture waiting to be explored.

Luang Prabang

Luang Prabang, a UNESCO World Heritage site, gives a peek into Laos's spiritual soul. Walk through narrow alleys with old buildings and golden temples, immersing yourself in a mix of old customs and the pulse of modern life.

Natural Wonders

Beyond the cities, Laos shows its natural wonders. Imagine green rice fields stretching to the horizon, tall mountains making a dramatic backdrop, and waterfalls cascading with a rhythm that echoes the country's heartbeat.

The Plain of Jars

The Plain of Jars, an archaeological puzzle, invites you to solve its mysteries. Ancient stone vessels scattered across the land hold stories from times long ago, adding a sense of mystery to your journey.

Four Thousand Islands

For those wanting peace, the Four Thousand Islands in the south provide a quiet haven. Here, the Mekong River becomes a network of islands, offering a retreat where time seems to stand still.

Yet, Laos is not just a landscape; it's a composition of smiles and warmth.

- ***The people, with their genuine hospitality***, welcome you into a world where the simple joys of life take center stage.

As you go through the pages of this guide, get ready to find the hidden gems of Laos – the must-visit places, the flavors of Laotian food, and the lively festivals that mark the calendar.

- ***Each chapter*** will reveal a new side of this captivating land, inviting you to start an adventure that will leave a mark on your travel memories.
- ***Laos calls***, ready to share its beauty and secrets with the curious explorer in you.

20 Fun-facts

1. The Land of a Million Elephants:

Laos's name translates to "The Land of a Million Elephants," symbolizing the deep historical significance of these majestic creatures in Lao culture.

2. A French Legacy:

Laos's colonial past has left an indelible mark on its architecture, particularly in Luang Prabang, where charming French colonial buildings line the streets.

3. World's Largest Bamboo Bridge:

Spanning a staggering 1,600 meters, the Kok Bridge in Luang Namtha is the world's longest suspension bridge made entirely of bamboo.

4. Home to the Hmong:

The Hmong people, renowned for their intricate needlework and deep connection to nature, are one of Laos's most colorful ethnic groups.

5. Sticky Rice Staple:

Khao Niao, or sticky rice, is a staple in Lao cuisine, often eaten with the hands and paired with various savory and spicy dishes.

6. Birthplace of Patuxay:

Vientiane, Laos's capital, is home to the Patuxay monument, a striking arch inspired by the Arc de Triomphe in Paris.

7. Serene Floating Villages:

The tranquil waters of Tonle Sap Lake are dotted with floating villages, offering a glimpse into the unique lifestyle of local fishermen and their families.

8. A Haven for Coffee Lovers:

Laos is home to some of the world's finest coffee beans, with the Bolaven Plateau region renowned for its Arabica and Robusta varieties.

9.   The Boun Festival:

Held annually during the dry season, the Boun Festival is a vibrant celebration of Lao culture, featuring colorful parades, traditional dances, and lively festivities.

10. A Slow-Paced Lifestyle:

Laos embraces the philosophy of Sabai dee, emphasizing slowing down, enjoying the present moment, and finding joy in the simple things.

11. A Treasure Trove of Temples:

Laos is home to a wealth of ancient temples, including the awe-inspiring Vat Phou in Champasak, a UNESCO World Heritage site.

12. A Culinary Adventure:

Lao cuisine is a symphony of flavors, blending sweet, sour, salty, and spicy notes, creating a unique and tantalizing culinary experience.

13. A Haven for Nature Lovers:

Laos's lush landscapes, cascading waterfalls, and diverse wildlife provide ample opportunities for nature exploration and adventure.

14. A Land of Tradition and Modernity:

Laos seamlessly blends ancient traditions and modern aspirations, evident in its vibrant festivals, bustling markets, and emerging art scene.

15. A Destination for Sustainable Travel:

Laos is committed to sustainable tourism practices, offering eco-friendly accommodations and experiences that respect the environment and local communities.

16. A Place of Warm Hospitality:

The Lao people are renowned for their warm smiles, genuine hospitality, and welcoming spirit, making every interaction a heartwarming experience.

17. A Hidden Gem Awaiting Discovery:

Laos remains relatively untouched by mass tourism, offering a sense of authenticity and off-the-beaten-path adventure.

18. A Land of Unspoiled Beauty:

Laos's natural beauty is unspoiled, from its pristine forests and verdant mountains to its serene lakes and cascading waterfalls.

19. A Melting Pot of Ethnicities:

Laos is home to a rich tapestry of ethnic groups, each with their distinct traditions, languages, and customs, offering a glimpse into the country's cultural diversity.

20. A Land of Enchanting Festivals:

Throughout the year, Laos comes alive with a vibrant array of festivals, each showcasing the country's unique customs, music, and dance, providing a captivating cultural immersion.

"To understand Laos is to embrace the simplicity of life and appreciate the profound beauty found in the smallest moments."

- Dalai Lama

Chapter 1:
Historical Antecedent

To truly appreciate the essence of Laos, it's essential to embark on a journey through its rich and captivating history, a diversity woven with tales of ancient kingdoms, powerful dynasties, and the enduring spirit of its people.

The Kingdom of Lan Xang

Laos's historical narrative begins with the rise of the Kingdom of Lan Xang, meaning "The Land of a Million Elephants," a powerful empire that emerged in the 14th century.

- *Under the reign of its illustrious monarchs*, Lan Xang flourished, becoming a hub of trade and cultural exchange along the Silk Road, its influence extending across present-day Laos, Thailand, Myanmar, and Vietnam.

The Khmer Influence

Laos's history is intertwined with that of the Khmer Empire, a powerful civilization that dominated Southeast Asia from the 9th to the 15th centuries.

- *The Khmer influence is evident in Laos's* architectural marvels, such as the awe-inspiring ruins of Vat Phou in Champasak, a UNESCO World Heritage site, and the intricate carvings at Wat Si Saket in Vientiane.

The Colonial Period

In the late 19th century, Laos fell under French colonial rule, a period that brought about significant changes to the country's landscape and social structures.

- *French colonial architecture*, particularly evident in Luang Prabang, stands as a testament to this era, while the introduction of new technologies and educational systems left a lasting impact on Lao society.

The Path to Independence

The struggle for independence from French colonial rule gained momentum in the mid-20th century, led by Lao nationalist movements.

- *In 1953, Laos finally regained its sovereignty*, marking a new chapter in the country's history.

The Modern Era

Since independence, Laos has undergone significant transformations, embracing modernization while striving to preserve its rich cultural heritage.

- *The country has made strides* in economic development and infrastructure improvement, while also promoting sustainable tourism practices that respect its natural beauty and cultural traditions.

A Legacy of Resilience and Spirit

Throughout its tumultuous history, Laos has demonstrated remarkable resilience and adaptability. Its people have preserved their cultural identity, their deep connection to the land, and their unwavering spirit.

13 Key Events In History:

1. **1353:** Founding of the Kingdom of Lan Xang

This is a powerful empire that unified much of present-day Laos and extended into parts of Thailand, Myanmar, and Vietnam.

2. **1545: Lan Xang at its Peak**

Lan Xang reaches its peak under King Setthathirath, who expands the kingdom's territory and promotes cultural and religious development.

3. **1778: Lan Xang breaks apart**

It break into three separate kingdoms: Vientiane, Luang Prabang, and Champasak. This period of division marks the beginning of Laos's decline.

4. **1893: Laos becomes a French protectorate**

This is the beginning of French colonial rule.

5. **1945: Japan occupies Laos during World War II**

It also grant the country nominal independence.

6. 1949: Laos gains full independence from France.

7. 1953: The Lao People's Revolutionary Party (LPRP)

It was established, marking the beginning of the country's communist movement.

8. 1954: The Geneva Accords

This ended the First Indochina War and divide Laos into three zones: a communist-controlled north, a neutral zone, and a royalist south.

9. 1960-1975: Laos becomes a battleground

It was a battleground in the Vietnam War, with the LPRP fighting a protracted civil war against the royalist government and its American allies.

10. 1975: The LPRP in total control

It took control of the entire country, establishing the Lao People's Democratic Republic.

11. 1991: Laos introduces economic reforms

Economic reformation and transitions to a market-oriented economy.

12. 2009: Laos joined WHO

It became a part of World Trade Organization (WTO).

13. 2016: Laos hosts the 10th ASEAN Summit

It showcased its growing role in regional and international affairs.

"The charm of Laos lies in its ability to make time stand still, allowing you to savor each moment."

- Tiziano Terzani

Chapter 2:
The Best Time Of The Year To Visit

To truly immerse yourself in the essence of this enchanting kingdom, it's essential to choose the most suitable time to visit, aligning your journey with the rhythm of the seasons and the unique experiences each period has to offer.

The Dry Season: (November-April)

As the rains gently subside and the sun casts its golden glow upon the land, Laos transforms into a haven for nature enthusiasts and culture seekers alike.

- *The dry season*, spanning from November to April, presents the ideal conditions for exploring the country's diverse landscapes, from trekking through verdant hills to navigating the meandering Mekong River.

- *During this period*, the skies are clear, the air is pleasantly crisp, and the humidity levels are low, making it a comfortable time to venture into the heart of Laos's natural wonders.

  - *The Bolaven Plateau,* with its cascading waterfalls and lush coffee plantations, unveils its breathtaking beauty, while the serene waters of Tonle Sap Lake invite you to witness the unique lifestyle of its floating villages.

- *The dry season also coincides* with a host of vibrant festivals that showcase Laos's rich cultural heritage.
  - *The Boun Festival*, held annually during this time, fills the streets with colorful parades, traditional dances, and lively festivities, offering a glimpse into the heart and soul of the Lao people.

The Shoulder Seasons: (October and May)

As the seasons transition between the wet and dry periods, Laos experiences a brief shoulder season, offering a unique blend of pleasant weather and fewer crowds.

- *October and May present* a delightful opportunity to explore the country without the peak season rush, allowing you to immerse yourself in the tranquility of its natural landscapes and cultural gems.

- *During this time*, the rains begin to taper off, providing a refreshing respite from the heat, while the skies still offer ample sunshine for outdoor adventures.
  - *The verdant hills and lush valleys* are at their most vibrant, adorned with a vibrant tapestry of wildflowers and greenery.

- *The shoulder seasons also offer* a more affordable option for travel, with accommodation prices and transportation costs generally lower than during the peak season.
  - *This makes it an ideal time* for budget-conscious travelers to discover the treasures of Laos without compromising on their experiences.

The Rainy Season: (June-September)

While the rainy season, extending from June to September, may deter some travelers, it unveils a different facet of Laos's enchanting beauty.

- *The abundant rainfall transforms* the landscape into a verdant paradise, with waterfalls cascading at their fullest, rivers swelling with life, and the air filled with the refreshing scent of petrichor.

- *This season offers a unique opportunity* to witness the raw power and beauty of nature.
  - *Trekking through the rain-soaked* forests unveils a hidden world of lush flora and fauna, while boat rides along the swollen Mekong River provide a glimpse into the resilience and adaptability of the local communities.

- *The rainy season also coincides* with the rice harvest, a time of celebration and gratitude for the bounty of the land.
  - *Witnessing the traditional methods* of rice cultivation and participating in the harvest festivals offers a deeper understanding of the Lao people's connection to nature and their agricultural heritage.

Choosing Your Ideal Time to Visit

The best time to visit Laos depends on your individual preferences and travel goals.

- ***Whether you seek the adventure of the dry season***, the tranquility of the shoulder seasons, or the raw beauty of the rainy season, each period offers unique experiences that will enrich your Laotian journey.

Embrace the essence of Sabai dee, the Lao philosophy of slowing down and savoring the moment. Let the beauty of Laos unfold before you, guided by the rhythm of the seasons and the spirit of discovery.

"To travel through Laos is to step into a living poetry, where each step is a verse in the ballad of the Mekong."

- Pico Iyer

Chapter 3:
How To Arrive and Move Like a Pro

As you embark on your Laotian adventure, the first step is to navigate the arrival procedures with ease, ensuring a smooth transition from the world outside to the enchanting realm of Laos.

Visa Requirements and Procedures

Most nationalities can obtain a visa on arrival at Luang Prabang International Airport or major land border crossings.

To ensure a hassle-free process, it's advisable to have the necessary documents ready:

- *A valid passport* with at least six months remaining validity
- *One recent passport*-sized photo
- *A visa application form*, which can be obtained at the visa window at Lao ports of entry or given before landing if you are arriving by plane
- *Visa fee* (in cash) in US dollars

Once you have gathered these documents, proceed to the visa window upon arrival.

- *The visa application process* is typically straightforward, and you'll receive your visa within minutes.

Baggage Claim and Customs Clearance

After collecting your baggage from the designated carousel, proceed to the customs clearance area.

- *Laos has a relatively relaxed customs policy*, but it's essential to declare any prohibited or restricted items you may be carrying, such as weapons, drugs, or certain agricultural products.

- *If you have nothing to declare*, simply proceed through the 'green channel.' For items requiring declaration, approach the customs officer at the 'red channel' and present any relevant documentation.

Currency Exchange and Banking

The official currency of Laos is the Lao Kip (LAK). While US dollars are widely accepted, it's advisable to exchange some currency for local transactions.

- *Currency exchange counters are available* at the airport and in major cities. ATMs are also prevalent, but it's recommended to inform your bank of your travel plans to avoid any card blockages.

Accommodation Options

Laos offers a wide range of accommodation options to suit every traveler's budget and preference.

- *From budget-friendly guesthouses* to luxurious hotels, you'll find a haven that matches your style and comfort level.

Moving From The Airport To The City

Whether you're arriving in the charming town of Luang Prabang or the bustling capital of Vientiane, there are a variety of convenient and affordable transportation options to connect you to your destination.

Luang Prabang International Airport

Situated just 4 kilometers from the UNESCO World Heritage town of Luang Prabang, Luang Prabang International Airport serves as the gateway to northern Laos.

- *Upon landing*, you'll find a range of transportation options awaiting you:

Taxi:

Taxis are readily available outside the terminal building.

- *Negotiate the fare clearly* before embarking on your journey, typically around 50,000 to 80,000 LAK (approximately US$5-8).

Tuk-tuk:

These three-wheeled vehicles offer a fun and affordable way to reach your hotel or guesthouse within the town center.

- *Expect to pay around 20,000* to 30,000 LAK (approximately US$2-3) for a short ride.

Shared Minivan:

For a more economical option, consider sharing a minivan with other passengers.

- *These minivans depart regularly* from the airport to the town center, costing around 15,000 to 20,000 LAK (approximately US$1.50-2) per person.

Wattay International Airport (Vientiane)

Located about 15 kilometers from Vientiane's city center, Wattay International Airport is the main gateway to central Laos.

- *Upon arrival,* you'll find several transportation options to suit your needs:

Taxi:

Taxis are plentiful outside the terminal building.

● *Negotiate the fare clearly before* starting your journey, typically around 100,000 to 150,000 LAK (approximately US$10-15).

Tuk-tuk:

While not as common as in Luang Prabang, tuk-tuks can be found at the airport, offering a more adventurous ride to your destination.

● *Expect to pay around 30,000* to 50,000 LAK (approximately US$3-5) for a short trip.

Airport Shuttle Bus:

For a convenient and cost-effective option, consider taking the airport shuttle bus. It operates from the airport to the city center, making stops at major hotels and landmarks.

● *The fare is around 20,000* LAK (approximately US$2) per person.

4 Tips for Getting Around

1. Exchange Currency:

Before leaving the airport, it's advisable to exchange some currency for local transactions. US dollars are widely accepted, but having some Lao Kip (LAK) will be handy for smaller purchases.

2. Agree on Fares in Advance:

Whether opting for a taxi or tuk-tuk, negotiate the fare clearly before starting your journey. This will help avoid any misunderstandings or disputes later.

3. Have Your Destination Address Ready:

Keep your hotel or guesthouse address handy to communicate clearly with your driver or ticketing staff.

4. Embrace the Sabai Dee Spirit:

Laos is known for its relaxed pace of life, so embrace the spirit of Sabai dee, meaning "slow down and enjoy the moment." Savor the journey from the airport to the city, taking in the sights and sounds of this enchanting country.

"Laos is a treasure trove of cultural gems, where traditions are not relics but living expressions of a vibrant heritage."

- Paulo Coelho

Chapter 4:
Culture and Tradition

The Lao people, known for their warm smiles and genuine hospitality, have preserved their heritage through a rich array of customs, beliefs, and artistic expressions.

Religious Beliefs

Theravada Buddhism is the predominant religion in Laos, deeply influencing the country's cultural landscape.

- *Golden temples and saffron-robed monks* grace the streets, while the principles of mindfulness and compassion permeate daily life.

- *Alongside Buddhism*, animism, the belief in spirits inhabiting natural objects, remains deeply rooted in Lao culture.

- *Shrines and offerings dot the countryside*, reflecting the reverence for the spirit world.

Festivals and Celebrations

Laos is a land of vibrant festivals that bring communities together in a symphony of colors, music, and dance.

- **The Boun Festival**, held annually during the dry season, is a colorful combination of parades, traditional performances, and lively celebrations, showcasing the country's rich cultural heritage.

- **The annual Boat Racing Festival** in Luang Prabang is a thrilling spectacle, with colorful dragon boats vying for victory along the mighty Mekong River.

Traditional Arts and Crafts

Laos boasts a rich tradition of arts and crafts, passed down through generations of artisans.

- *Weaving,* particularly the intricate silk textiles known as pha sin, is a cornerstone of Lao craftsmanship.

- *Silverwork,* wood carving, and lacquerware are also highly prized, each showcasing the dexterity and artistry of Lao artisans.

Cuisine

Lao cuisine is an enticing blend of flavors, reflecting the country's diverse cultural influences.

- **Sticky rice**, a staple in Lao cuisine, is often eaten with the hands, accompanied by a variety of savory and spicy dishes.

- **Tam mak hoong**, a spicy papaya salad, is a national favorite, while khao soi, a coconut curry noodle soup, showcases French culinary influences.

Family and Social Values

Family and community play a central role in Lao society.

- *Elders are revered* for their wisdom and experience, while younger generations are expected to show respect and deference.

- *The concept of Sabai dee*, emphasizing slowing down and savoring the present moment, permeates daily life, creating a relaxed and harmonious atmosphere.

Language and Etiquette

The Lao language, a member of the Tai-Kadai family, is the official language of Laos.

- *While learning a few basic phrases* will enhance your interactions, English is increasingly spoken in tourist areas.

- *Cultural sensitivity is essential,* especially when visiting temples or attending ceremonies.

- *Dress modestly,* remove shoes before entering sacred spaces, and avoid pointing with your feet or touching the head of others.

A Culture in Harmony with Nature

The Lao people have a deep connection to the natural world, evident in their reverence for the Mekong River, their sustainable agricultural practices, and their belief in the spirit world residing within nature.

- *This harmonious relationship* with the environment is an integral part of Lao culture and identity.

10 Important Dates and Celebrations

1. Boun Pha Wet (January)

Boun Pha Wet, also known as the Rocket Festival, is a vibrant celebration held in January to commemorate the birth, enlightenment, and death of Lord Buddha.

2. Boun Khao Chi (February)

Boun Khao Chi, or the Rice Ceremony, is a traditional Lao festival held in February to honor the rice spirit and ensure a successful harvest.

3. Lao New Year (Pi Mai)

Lao New Year, also known as Pi Mai, is a joyous celebration held in April to mark the beginning of the Lao solar calendar.

4. Boun Visakha (May)

Boun Visakha, or the Full Moon Festival, is a significant Buddhist celebration held in May to commemorate the birth, enlightenment, and death of Lord Buddha.

5. Boun Bang Fai (May-September)

Boun Bang Fai, or the Rocket Festival, is a vibrant celebration held in various villages throughout Laos between May and September to call for good rain and a bountiful harvest.

6. Boun Khao Phansa (July)

Boun Khao Phansa, or the Start of Buddhist Lent, marks the beginning of the three-month Buddhist rainy season in July.

7. Boun Khao Salak (September)

Boun Khao Salak, or the Rice Planting Ceremony, is a traditional Lao festival held in September to mark the beginning of the rice planting season.

8. Boun Ok (Awk) Phansa (October)

Boun Ok (Awk) Phansa, or the End of Buddhist Lent, marks the end of the three-month Buddhist rainy season in October.

9. That Luang Festival (November)

The That Luang Festival, held in November, is a grand celebration of Laos's most sacred stupa, That Luang, located in Vientiane.

- *The festival features colorful parades*, traditional dances, and lively revelry, attracting visitors from across Laos and beyond.

10. Lao National Day (December)

Lao National Day, celebrated on December 2nd, commemorates the day Laos regained independence from France in 1949.

- *During this national holiday*, government offices are closed, and public celebrations may take place, such as flag-raising ceremonies and cultural performances.

"In the heart of Laos, time slows down, and the whispers of ancient spirits echo in the breeze."

- Isabella Bird

Chapter 5:
How To Get The Best Accommodation

Laos offers a diverse array of accommodation options to suit every traveler's style and budget. Whether you seek the tranquility of a riverside retreat, the charm of a traditional Lao guesthouse, or the modern comforts of a luxury hotel, Laos has a haven waiting for you.

5 Best Hotels and Resorts

1. Rosewood Luang Prabang:

Nestled in the heart of Luang Prabang's UNESCO World Heritage Town, Rosewood Luang Prabang is a luxurious retreat that seamlessly blends contemporary design with traditional Lao architecture.

● *Overlooking the serene Nam Khan River*, the hotel offers guests a tranquil oasis amidst the vibrant city.

Contact: +856 71 211 155

Email: luangprabang@rosewoodhotels.com

Website: www.rosewoodhotels.com/en/luang-prabang

Rating: 4.6/5.0

2. La Résidence Phou Vao:

Formerly the residence of a French governor, La Résidence Phou Vao is a charming boutique hotel exuding a colonial elegance that transports guests back in time.

- *Located on a hilltop overlooking* Luang Prabang, the hotel offers panoramic views of the city and surrounding mountains.

Contact: +856 71 212530

Website:

https://www.belmond.com/hotels/asia/laos/luang-praban g/belmond-la-residence-phou-vao

Rating: 4.3/5.0

3. Sofitel Luang Prabang:

Situated on the banks of the Mekong River, Sofitel Luang Prabang is a modern hotel that harmoniously blends French luxury with Lao cultural influences.

- *The hotel features a stunning infinity pool* overlooking the river, a world-class spa, and a variety of dining options.

Contact: +856 71 260 777

Email: h9669-re@sofitel.com

Website:

https://all.accor.com/hotel/9669/index.en.shtml

Rating: 4.6/5.0

4. The Luang Say Residence:

Located in the heart of Luang Prabang's UNESCO World Heritage Town, The Luang Say Residence is a collection of beautifully restored traditional Lao houses that offer a unique and intimate accommodation experience.

● *The hotel features a serene courtyard pool*, an award-winning restaurant, and personalized service.

Contact: +856 71 260 891

Email: rsvn@luangsayresidence.la

Website: https://www.luangsayresidence.la/

Rating: 4.4/5.0

5. Satri House:

Nestled in a quiet corner of Luang Prabang's UNESCO World Heritage Town, Satri House is a charming boutique hotel that exudes a tranquil and inviting atmosphere.

- *The hotel features a beautiful courtyard pool*, a rooftop bar with panoramic views, and a blend of traditional Lao and contemporary design.

Contact: +856 71 253 491-2

Email: info@satrihouse.com

Website: http://www.satrihouse.com/

Rating: 4.6/5.0

5 Best Budget Hotels

1. The Gibbon Experience:

Nestled in the Bokeo province of northern Laos, The Gibbon Experience offers a unique and affordable jungle adventure. With its treetop cabins, ziplines, and breathtaking views of the Nam Khan River, this eco-friendly accommodation provides an unforgettable experience for budget-conscious travelers seeking a taste of the Laotian wilderness.

Contact: +856 30 57 45 866

Email: info@gibbonexperience.org

Website: https://www.gibbonexperience.org/

Rating: 4.6/5.0

2. The Sanctuary Hostel Luang Prabang:

Situated in the serene UNESCO World Heritage Town of Luang Prabang, The Sanctuary Hostel Luang Prabang offers a tranquil oasis amidst the city's vibrant charm. With its comfortable dorms, shared facilities, and rooftop terrace overlooking the Nam Khan River, this hostel provides a peaceful haven for budget travelers.

Contact: +856 71 213 777

Website: www.sanctuaryhotelsandresorts.com/english/

Rating: 4.4/5.0

3. Vansana Homestay Luang Prabang:

Immerse yourself in the heart of Lao culture by staying at Vansana Homestay Luang Prabang. This family-run homestay offers a unique opportunity to experience local hospitality, and enjoy home-cooked meals.

Contact: +856 21 252 090

Website: http://www.vansanahotel-group.com/

Rating: 3.9/5.0

4. Namkhan Riverside Hotel:

Situated on the banks of the Nam Khan River in Luang Prabang, It offers a tranquil and affordable retreat. With its riverside bungalows, shared facilities, and friendly staff, this guesthouse provides a relaxing haven for budget travelers seeking a peaceful escape.

Contact: +856 20 92 188 665

Rating: 4.4/5.0

5. DokPhut Guesthouse:

Located in the heart of Vang Vieng, DokPhut Guesthouse offers a relaxed and social atmosphere, perfect for backpackers and budget-conscious travelers.

- **With its spacious dorms**, shared facilities, and friendly staff, this guesthouse is a great place to connect with fellow travelers and experience the town's vibrant energy.

Contact: +856 20 99 716 551

Rating: 5.0/5.0

10 Keys to a Suitable Accommodation

1. Consider your budget:

Accommodation in Laos ranges from budget-friendly hostels to luxurious resorts and boutique hotels.

- *Determine your budget* and look for options that fit within your price range.

2. Define your travel style:

Are you a solo traveler seeking a social atmosphere, or a couple looking for a romantic getaway?

- *Do you prefer to be in the heart* of the action or surrounded by nature?

Laos offers a variety of accommodation options to suit different travel styles.

3. Choose a convenient location:

Consider the location of your accommodation in relation to your desired activities and interests.

- *If you plan to explore the city center*, it might be ideal to be within walking distance of major attractions.

- *If you're seeking a tranquil retreat*, consider staying in a quiet village or amidst the natural beauty of the countryside.

4. Consider the amenities:

What amenities are important to you?

- *Do you need a private bathroom*, air conditioning, Wi-Fi access, or a swimming pool?
- *Make a list of your must-have amenities* and look for accommodation that provides them.

5. Read reviews:

Before booking your accommodation, take some time to read reviews from other travelers.

- *This can give you valuable insights* into the quality of the accommodation, the staff, and the overall experience.

6. Book in advance:

During peak season, accommodation in Laos can fill up quickly, especially in popular tourist destinations.

- *Book your accommodation* in advance to ensure you get the best options and prices.

7. Consider homestay options:

Homestays offer a unique opportunity to experience Lao culture and hospitality firsthand.

- *You'll get to live like a local*, learn about their traditions, and enjoy home-cooked meals.

8. Bargain for a better price:

Bargaining is a common practice in Laos, especially in smaller towns and villages.

- *Don't be afraid to negotiate* the price of your accommodation, especially if you're staying for multiple nights.

9. Be flexible:

Sometimes, the best deals on accommodation can be found by being flexible with your dates and arrival times.

- If you're open to these possibilities, you might be able to save money or find a more unique accommodation option.

10. Embrace the Lao spirit of Sabai Dee:

Laos is a laid-back country with a relaxed atmosphere.

- *Embrace the spirit of Sabai Dee*, which means "slow down and enjoy the moment."
- *Don't stress about finding* the perfect accommodation, just let the process flow and enjoy the journey.

"Laos, a land where time becomes a storyteller, narrating tales of resilience and tranquility."

- Khalil Gibran

Chapter 6:
Must-See Attraction Spots

From ancient temples to serene waterfalls, vibrant markets to karst mountains, Laos offers a goldmine of experiences that will leave you spellbound.

10 Must-See Sites

1. Luang Prabang: A UNESCO World Heritage Town

Step back in time as you wander through the UNESCO World Heritage Town of Luang Prabang, where ancient temples and colonial-era architecture seamlessly blend with the charm of modern-day life.

2. Kuang Si Falls: A Cascading Paradise

Immerse yourself in the serene beauty of Kuang Si Falls, a three-tiered waterfall cascading amidst lush greenery.

- *Hike through the verdant forest* and discover turquoise pools, hidden caves, and cascading waterfalls.

3. Vang Vieng: A Haven for Adventure Seekers

Venture into the heart of Vang Vieng, a town nestled amidst towering karst mountains and the Nam Song River.

4. The Plain of Jars: A Mystery Unraveled

Journey to the enigmatic Plain of Jars, a vast plateau scattered with thousands of mysterious stone jars.

5. Pak Ou Caves: A Sanctuary of Buddha Images

Venture into the heart of the Tham Pak Ou Caves, a sacred site revered by Lao people.

6. The Bolaven Plateau: A Coffee Lover's Paradise

Explore the verdant expanses of the Bolaven Plateau, a region renowned for its rich volcanic soil and vibrant coffee culture.

7. Tat Kuang Si: A Hidden Waterfall Gem

Venture off the beaten path to discover Tat Kuang Si, a hidden waterfall nestled amidst lush greenery.

8. Vientiane: A Capital City with a Laid-Back Charm

Immerse yourself in the relaxed atmosphere of Vientiane, the capital city of Laos.

- *Visit the iconic Patuxay*, a triumphal arch inspired by the Arc de Triomphe in Paris.

9. Nam Khan River: A Tranquil Escape

Escape the hustle and bustle of the city and embark on a leisurely boat ride along the Nam Khan River.

- *Float through the serene waters*, passing by lush greenery and traditional Lao villages.

10. Vieng Xai: A Gateway to the Hidden North

Venture into the heart of Vieng Xai, a town nestled amidst the mountains of northern Laos.

- *Explore the vibrant local markets*, discover hidden waterfalls, and immerse yourself in the rich cultural heritage of the region.

"Laos teaches us that true wealth lies not in possessions but in the richness of the human spirit."

- Anne Morrow Lindbergh

Chapter 7:
Food and Drink

From spicy salads and savory soups to fresh spring rolls and delectable desserts, Lao cuisine is a symphony of flavors that will tantalize your taste buds and leave you craving for more.

10 Must Taste Cuisine

1. Sticky Rice: The Staple of Lao Cuisine

Sticky rice, known as "khao niao," is the foundation of Lao cuisine, forming the base of many dishes and eaten with both hands.

- *This glutinous rice* is steamed in bamboo baskets, giving it a unique texture and aroma that pairs perfectly with the spicy and savory flavors of Lao food.

2. Laap: A Minced Meat Salad Combination

Laap, a minced meat salad, is a staple of Lao cuisine and a must-try for any visitor.

- *This dish is typically made with minced pork*, beef, or chicken, mixed with shallots, garlic, chili peppers, and fish sauce, creating a composition of flavors that is both spicy and savory.

3. Tam Mak Houng: A Green Papaya Salad Sensation

Tam Mak Houng, a green papaya salad, is another popular dish in Laos.

- *This refreshing salad is made with unripe* green papaya, shredded carrots, tomatoes, and peanuts, all tossed in a dressing of fish sauce, lime juice, and chili peppers.
  - *The combination of textures* and flavors is both surprising and delightful.

4. Khao Soi: A Noodly Delight

Khao soi, a noodle soup, is a popular dish in northern Laos, particularly in Luang Prabang.

- *This dish features thick egg noodles* topped with a rich and savory curry broth, often containing chicken or beef, and served with a side of crispy shallots and pickled cabbage.

5. Sai Oua: A Sausage with a Difference

Sai Oua, a grilled sausage, is a unique Lao specialty. This sausage is made with minced pork, rice noodles, herbs, and spices, and then wrapped in banana leaves and grilled to perfection.

- *The result is a flavorful and aromatic sausage* that is both savory and slightly sweet.

6. Or Lam: A Sweet and Sticky Treat

Or Lam, a steamed sticky rice dessert, is a sweet and satisfying end to a Lao meal.

- *This dish is made with sticky rice*, coconut milk, and palm sugar, and often served with a topping of fresh bananas or jackfruit.
- *The combination of textures* and flavors is both comforting and delightful.

7.Khao Jee Paté (Baguette Sandwich):

A French-Lao Fusion Laos's colonial past has left an indelible mark on its cuisine, and khao jee paté is a prime example of this fusion.

- *This baguette sandwich is a popular street food*, combining crispy French bread with a flavorful pâté filling. The pâté is typically made with pork or liver, and it's seasoned with a variety of spices, giving it a rich and savory flavor.

8. Khao Piak Sen (Wet Noodle Soup):

On a chilly evening or after a long day exploring, there's nothing more comforting than a bowl of khao piak sen.

- *This wet noodle soup is a Lao staple*, featuring thin rice noodles in a flavorful broth.

9. Fresh Fruit Shakes: A Tropical Refreshment

Fresh fruit shakes are a refreshing and healthy way to quench your thirst in Laos. Made with a variety of tropical fruits, such as mangoes, papayas, and bananas.

10. Coffee: A Morning Ritual

Coffee is a popular beverage in Laos, and morning rituals often involve enjoying a cup of strong, dark coffee.

- *Lao coffee* is typically made with robusta beans.

5 Best Place to Eat

1. Tamarind, Luang Prabang

Nestled amidst the tranquil streets of Luang Prabang, Tamarind offers a refined dining experience that showcases Lao cuisine at its finest. Savor the delicate flavors of their signature Tamarind Fish, or delight in the aromatic notes of their Lemongrass-Infused Chicken.

Contact: +856 71 213 128

Email: info@tamarindlaos.com

Website: https://www.tamarindlaos.com/

Rating: 4.4/5.0

2. La Terrasse du Café, Luang Prabang

Embrace the charm of colonial Laos at La Terrasse du Café, a timeless establishment overlooking the Mekong River. Indulge in a leisurely breakfast of pastries and coffee, or savor a classic French meal amidst the elegant ambiance.

Contact: +856 21 218 550

Rating: 4.5/5.0

3. Bamboo Garden, Luang Prabang

Immerse yourself in the authentic flavors of Lao cuisine at Bamboo Garden, where traditional dishes are prepared with fresh, local ingredients.

- *Their signature Khao Soi*, a rich and flavorful noodle soup, is a must-try.

Contact: +856 20 97 188 899

Website:

https://bamboogardenluangprabang.business.site/

Rating: 4.7/5.0

4. Friends' Restaurant, Vang Vieng

Escape the bustle of Vang Vieng's riverside bars and discover Friends' Restaurant, a local gem offering authentic Lao cuisine.

- *Their Tam Mak Houng*, a green papaya salad, is a refreshing and flavorful treat.

Contact: +856 20 99 923 595

Rating: 4.5/5.0

5. Bamboo Tree Restaurant, Vientiane:

Step into a world of culinary excellence at Bamboo Tree Restaurant, a Vientiane institution known for its refined Lao cuisine. Their signature Laap, a minced meat salad, is a must-try for any food enthusiast.

Contact: +856 20 22 425 499

Rating: 4.3/5.0

6 Tips for Choosing the Right Restaurant

1. Consider your location and budget:

Determine your budget and choose a restaurant that fits within your price range. Consider the location of the restaurant in relation to your desired activities and interests.

2. Check reviews and recommendations:

Before booking your reservation, take some time to read reviews from other travelers. This can give you valuable insights into the quality of the food, the staff, and the overall experience.

3. Consider the type of cuisine you're craving:

Laos offers a variety of cuisines, from traditional Lao dishes to international fare.

- *If you're seeking an authentic* Lao experience, look for restaurants that specialize in local cuisine.
- *If you're craving a taste of home* or are looking for something more familiar, there are plenty of options for international cuisine.

4. Check for dietary restrictions:

If you have any dietary restrictions, be sure to check the restaurant's menu or call ahead to inquire about their options.

- *Many restaurants in Laos* can accommodate vegetarian, vegan, and gluten-free diets.

5. Consider the ambiance and atmosphere:

The ambiance of a restaurant can significantly impact your dining experience.

- *If you're looking for a lively* and social atmosphere, choose a restaurant with an outdoor seating placement.

- *If you prefer a more intimate and relaxed setting,* opt for a quieter restaurant with cozy lighting and comfortable seating.

6. Look for seasonal specialties and fresh ingredients:

Laos offers a bounty of fresh, seasonal ingredients throughout the year.

- *Ask about the restaurant's signature* dishes or seasonal specialties.

"In Laos, the beauty is not just in the scenery but in the unhurried pace of life."

- Elizabeth Gilbert

Chapter 8:
Recreational and Fun Activities

From exploring ancient temples to immersing yourself in vibrant markets, Laos offers a treasure trove of experiences that will leave you spellbound. But amidst these cultural wonders, Laos also unveils a world of recreational adventures, catering to every taste and budget.

The 10 Best To Do Things

1. Explore Luang Prabang's Streets:

Walk around the cool streets of Luang Prabang, a UNESCO World Heritage site. Check out the old buildings, shiny temples, and lively markets that make this city a living proof of Laos's rich culture.

2. Ride the Mekong River at Sunset:

Take a calm boat ride along the Mekong River as the sun paints the sky with colors. Look at the peaceful water and the pretty scenes along the riverbanks.

3. Check Out the Plain of Jars:

Solve the mysteries of the Plain of Jars, an old place full of stories. Explore the big landscape with huge stone jars, each holding secrets from a long time ago.

4. Join a Laotian Festival:

Be part of the fun at a Laotian festival. From the wet fun of Songkran to the bright processions of Boun Ok Phansa, these celebrations let you feel the joy and culture of Laos.

5. Hike Through Luang Namtha:

Put on your hiking shoes and go into the green areas of Luang Namtha. Hike through thick forests, see small villages, and watch the different plants and animals that make northern Laos beautiful.

6. See Vang Vieng's Karst Landscapes:

Explore the pretty karst landscapes of Vang Vieng, where tall cliffs make a cool backdrop. Go on a river adventure, explore caves, and enjoy the awesome scenery.

7. Visit Wat Phu Temple Complex:

Go back in time at the Wat Phu temple complex, a cool example of Khmer architecture. Look at the detailed carvings and walk around the special grounds with ancient rituals.

8. Enjoy Laotian Cuisine:

Treat yourself to the tastes of Laotian food. From tasty street food to special dishes in local places, enjoy the mix of herbs and spices that make Laotian cooking unique.

9. Hang Out with Elephants in Sayaboury:

Feel the power of elephants in Sayaboury. Get close to them in a good way, learn about saving them, and see these big animals in their natural home.

10. Chill in the Four Thousand Islands:

Relax in the quiet Four Thousand Islands in southern Laos. Find out about the slow life on these river islands, where the Mekong River spreads out into peaceful spots.

10 Best Romantic Getaways for Couples

1. Sunset at Wat Xieng Thong

As the sun begins its descent, casting a golden glow over the city, make your way to Wat Xieng Thong, Luang Prabang's oldest temple. Hand in hand, wander through the serene temple grounds, savoring the tranquility of the moment.

2. Morning Alms Ceremony

Rise early and immerse yourselves in the spiritual beauty of the morning alms ceremony, a daily ritual that takes place in every Lao town and village.

3. Hot Air Balloon Ride

Soar above the enchanting landscapes of Luang Prabang in a hot air balloon ride, an experience that promises breathtaking views and a touch of romance.

- ***As you float gently through the air***, witness the city's golden temples, the meandering Mekong River, and the lush greenery that surrounds the town.

4. Private Cooking Class

Embark on a culinary adventure together by taking a private cooking class, where you can learn the secrets of Lao cuisine under the guidance of a local chef.

- *Hand in hand*, prepare a traditional Lao meal, savoring the flavors and aromas that will tantalize your taste buds.

5. Sunset Cruise on the Mekong River

As the sun dips below the horizon, casting a warm glow over the Mekong River, embark on a romantic sunset cruise. Sip on refreshing cocktails, enjoy a delectable picnic basket, and soak in the breathtaking views of the river.

6. Kuang Si Waterfall

Escape the hustle and bustle of the city and immerse yourselves in the enchanting beauty of Kuang Si Waterfall, a three-tiered masterpiece cascading amidst lush greenery.

- *Hand in hand*, hike through the verdant forest, discovering turquoise pools, hidden caves, and cascading waterfalls.

7. Traditional Lao Massage

Unwind together and indulge in a traditional Lao massage, a deeply relaxing and restorative experience.

- *Experienced therapists* will soothe away your tensions, leaving you feeling refreshed and revitalized.
- *Emerge from the massage* feeling rejuvenated and ready to embrace the next stage of your romantic journey.

8. Private Picnic at Pha Tad Waterfall

Venturing off the beaten path, discover the serenity of Pha Tad Waterfall, a hidden gem nestled amidst the lush landscapes of Southern Laos.

- *Pack a picnic basket filled with local delicacies*, find a secluded spot amidst the rocks surrounding the waterfall, and enjoy a tranquil retreat together.

9. Explore Ancient Ruins

Embark on a journey through time together by exploring the ancient ruins of Vat Phou, a UNESCO World Heritage Site located in Champasak.

- *Wander through the remnants* of this once-thriving Khmer temple complex, imagining the grandeur of its past.

- *Hand in hand,* climb the ancient steps to the top of the temple ruins and marvel at the panoramic views of the surrounding countryside.

10. Stargazing in the Nam Khan River Valley

Escape the city lights and immerse yourselves in the enchanting beauty of the Nam Khan River Valley.

- *As darkness falls*, spread a blanket on the riverbank, lie down hand in hand, and gaze up at the celestial spectacle above.

- *Share whispered secrets* and dreams under the twinkling stars, creating a moment of pure intimacy and connection.

"Laos invites you to be a guest in its timeless story, where every chapter is a celebration of life's simple joys."

- Rumi

Chapter 9:
Shopping Activities

Beyond its natural beauty and ancient temples, Laos offers a goldmine of shopping experiences that will cater to every taste and budget. From bustling night markets to serene artisan villages.

The 10 Best Shopping Avenue/Market/Mall

1. Luang Prabang Night Market:

Step into the lively Luang Prabang's Night Market, open every evening. This market displays local crafts, textiles, and handmade items.

- ***Bargain with local sellers*** for special souvenirs that reflect Laos's culture.

2. Vientiane Morning Market:

Rise early to check out the busy Vientiane Morning Market. It's a paradise for bargain hunters, offering traditional fabrics and handmade jewelry.

- ***Explore narrow lanes to find hidden*** gems at affordable prices.

3. Talat Sao Mall:

For a mix of traditional and modern shopping, visit Talat Sao Mall in Vientiane. Explore stalls with clothing, electronics, and local snacks.

- *This mall suits different tastes*, making it a convenient stop for diverse shopping needs.

4. Ock Pop Tok Living Crafts Centre:

Dive into Laotian textiles at the Ock Pop Tok Living Crafts Centre in Luang Prabang. Discover handwoven fabrics dyed with natural methods.

- **The center not only offers** a unique shopping experience but also shares the ancient art of weaving.

5. Luang Namtha Night Market:

Experience the lively Luang Namtha Night Market, perfect for those seeking local products.

- *From handmade accessories to local treats*, this market captures northern Laos's essence and is ideal for budget-conscious travelers.

6. Dong Palan Silk Village:

Visit Dong Palan Silk Village near Vang Vieng, where traditional silk weaving is the focus.

- *Buy exquisite silk products* directly from the artisans, ensuring your souvenirs reflect Laotian craftsmanship.

7. Talat Khua Din Market, Pakse:

Explore the bustling Talat Khua Din Market in Pakse. This market offers a diverse range of goods, from fresh produce to handmade crafts.

- *Engage with local vendors* for a personalized shopping experience.

8. Namphou Fountain Mall:

For modern shopping in Vientiane, visit Namphou Fountain Mall.

- *This mall features local* and international brands, making it a suitable destination for those seeking a contemporary shopping experience.

9. Hmong Market, Phonsavan:

Discover Phonsavan's cultural richness at the Hmong Market. Run by the Hmong ethnic group, this market offers handmade textiles, traditional jewelry, and local produce.

- *Interact with sellers to learn* about the cultural significance of their crafts.

10. Old Quarter Market, Savannakhet:

Explore the charming Old Quarter Market in Savannakhet, with French colonial architecture as a backdrop.

- *This market is a goldmine of antiques*, handmade crafts, and local treats, making it an ideal stop for those seeking unique finds.

5 Key Tips for Shopping

1. Bargaining is essential.

Approach bargaining with a smile and a sense of humor, and be prepared to walk away if the price doesn't feel right.

- *Remember that the vendors are often* relying on these sales for their livelihoods, so be respectful and negotiate in a spirit of mutual understanding.

2. Support local artisans and fair trade initiatives.

Look for handicrafts and souvenirs that are made locally and support fair trade initiatives that empower local communities.

- *This is a great way to ensure* that your purchases are having a positive impact on the lives of the people who created them.

3. Consider the quality of the items you purchase.

Laos is known for its high-quality handicrafts, but there are also some imitations and low-quality items available.

- *Take your time to inspect the items* you are interested in and make sure they are made from good materials and are well-crafted.

4. Be aware of the rules and regulations regarding the export of antiques and cultural relics.

It is illegal to export certain antiques and cultural relics from Laos without a permit.

- *If you are interested in purchasing these items*, make sure to check with the authorities first.

5. Be patient and enjoy the experience.

Shopping in Laos is a leisurely affair. Don't rush through the process.

- *Take your time to browse the stalls*, chat with the vendors, and learn about the local handicrafts.

"To wander through Laos is to read a living poem, where nature, culture, and history coalesce in harmony."

- Elizabeth Lawrence

Chapter 10:
Language and Communication

The diverse linguistic landscape of Laos reflects the country's rich cultural diversity. Let's unravel the threads of language and communication to help you connect with the heart of this enchanting nation.

Lao Phrases for Everyday Interaction:

Embrace the warmth of Laotian culture by learning a few simple phrases. "Sabaidee" (hello) and "Khawp jai" (thank you) go a long way in sparking friendly exchanges with locals.

● *Simple gestures and greetings* can open doors to meaningful connections.

Language Diversity:

Laos boasts a mosaic of languages spoken by various ethnic groups. While Lao is the official language, you may encounter different dialects in rural areas. Engaging in basic communication demonstrates respect for the country's linguistic diversity.

Non-Verbal Communication:

Beyond words, non-verbal communication plays a crucial role in Laotian culture. A nod or a smile can convey sincerity and understanding.

- *Take cues from locals* and embrace the unspoken language that fosters connections beyond linguistic barriers.

Navigating Language Challenges:

In tourist hubs, English is commonly understood. However, in more remote areas, it's helpful to have a basic phrasebook. The effort to communicate in the local language is often appreciated and can lead to memorable encounters with the people of Laos.

Traditional Forms of Expression:

Explore the traditional arts of Laos, where storytelling is woven into various art forms.

- *From dance performances to intricate crafts*, each creation tells a story of the nation's history and cultural identity.

Marketplace Banter:

Engage in the lively banter of local markets, where bargaining is an art form. Politeness and a friendly demeanor go a long way in securing fair deals.

- *The market atmosphere provides* an excellent opportunity to practice your newfound language skills.

Interacting in Rural Communities:

If your journey takes you to rural areas, embrace the opportunity to connect with local communities. Simple greetings and an openness to local customs create bridges that transcend language barriers, allowing you to experience the heart of rural Laos.

Expressing Gratitude:

In Laos, expressing gratitude is a cornerstone of polite communication. Whether receiving a kind gesture or enjoying a delicious meal, a sincere "Khawp jai" conveys appreciation and leaves a positive impression on those you encounter.

Common Phrases and Expressions:

Familiarizing yourself with these phrases will not only enhance your travel experience but also help you connect with the friendly locals.

53 Common Expression and Phrases To Connect Like a Pro

Greetings and Basic Phrases

1. **Hello:** Sabai dii (pronounced sa-bye-dee)

2. **Goodbye:** Lae laan (pronounced lay-lahn)

3. **Thank you:** Khamphoui (pronounced kham-poui)

4. **You're welcome:** Chai dee (pronounced chai-dee)

5. **Please:** Bounthone (pronounced boon-tone)

6. **Excuse me:** Thoat khoua (pronounced tore-khoa)

7. **I don't understand:** Khai nyai (pronounced khyai-nye)

8. **Do you speak English?:** Phak Lao dai? (pronounced phak lao dye?)

9. **How much is this?:** Nee tua lai? (pronounced nee tua lye?)

Ordering Food and Drinks

10. **I want to eat:** Khao gin (pronounced khao gin)

11. **I want to drink:** Deum gin (pronounced deum gin)

12. **What is this?:** Nee men nyang? (pronounced nee men nyang?)

13. **I want to order:** Khao gin jai (pronounced khao gin jai)

14. **One, two, three:** Neung, song, sam (pronounced neung, song, sam)

15. **Water:** Nam (pronounced nahm)

16. **Coffee:** Kafe (pronounced kafeh)

Asking for Directions

17. **Where is the bathroom?:** Hong nam sai? (pronounced hong nahm sai?)

18. **Where is the...?:** Sai...bong? (pronounced sai...bong?)

19. **How can I get to...?:** Bonthi pen... dai? (pronounced bon-thi pen... dai?)

20. **Is it close?:** Pid bo? (pronounced pid bo?)

21. **Is it far?:** Kaai bo? (pronounced kai bo?)

22. **Straight ahead:** Tong dai (pronounced tong dai)

23. **Turn left:** Sai kway (pronounced sai kway)

24. **Turn right:** Sai baw (pronounced sai baw)

Shopping and Bargaining

25. **How much is this?:** Tow dai? (pronounced tow dai?)

26. **That's too expensive:** Peng lai (pronounced peng lai)

27. **Can you give me a discount?:** Lom lai dai? (pronounced lom lai dai?)

28. **I'll take it:** Jai lai (pronounced jai lai)

29. **No, thank you:** Baw, khop chai (pronounced baw, khop chai)

30. **Do you have...?:** Mee...bo? (pronounced mee...bo?)

31. **I'm looking for...:** Khao dorn... (pronounced khao dorn...)

Expressing Gratitude

32. **Thank you very much:** Khop jai lai lai (pronounced khop jai lai lai)

33. **I appreciate your help:** Khop jai khao tchaai (pronounced khop jai khao tchaai)

34. **You're very kind:** Jai pen khen dai (pronounced jai pen khen dai)

35. **Thank you for everything:** Khop jai souk (pronounced khop jai souk)

Emergency Situations

36. **Help!:** Chau dai! (pronounced chau dai!)

37. **Police:** Satanee tamluat (pronounced sa-ta-nee tam-luat)

38. **Hospital:** Hong maw (pronounced hong maw)

39. **Doctor:** Mor phaak (pronounced mor phak)

40. **I'm lost:** Khai pan (pronounced khyai pan)

41. **I'm sick:** Chai pen pen (pronounced chai pen pen)

Expressing Interest

42. **I'm interested in...:** Khao sai... (pronounced khao sai...)

43. **Tell me more about...:** Khao pan... (pronounced khao pan...)

44. **Can you show me...?:** Bong chai dai... (pronounced bong chai dai...)

45. **I'd like to buy...:** Khao sai soun... (pronounced khao sai soun...)

46. **Do you have any recommendations?:** Mee khao kao pan dai? (pronounced mee khao kao pan dai?)

47. **What is the best place to...?:** Bong sai dai pen... (pronounced bong sai dai pen...)

Making Friends

48. **Nice to meet you:** Tani dee (pronounced ta-nee dee)

49. **My name is...:** Khai pen... (pronounced khyai pen...)

50. **What is your name?:** Jao pen... (pronounced jao pen...)

51. **How are you?:** Sabaidee baw? (pronounced sa-bye-dee baw?)

52. **I'm from...:** Khai pen khon... (pronounced khyai pen khon...)

53. **I hope we can be friends:** Khao sai pen pen toon (pronounced khao sai pen pen toon)

10 Key Tips to Communicate Like A Pro

1. Learn a few basic Lao phrases:
Even a few simple phrases can go a long way in enhancing your interactions with locals and enriching your travel experience.

2. Embrace non-verbal communication cues:
Non-verbal communication plays a crucial role in Laos. The traditional Lao greeting, the "nop," involves placing both hands together in prayer position at the chest and bowing the head.

- *This gesture conveys respect*, gratitude, or requesting permission.

3. Respect the pace and style of Lao communication:
Laos is known for its laid-back atmosphere, and this extends to communication.

- *Take your time*, speak softly, and let conversations unfold naturally. Avoid rushing or using direct language.

4. Be mindful of cultural sensitivities:

Lao culture is steeped in respect and politeness. Avoid using direct or confrontational language, and always address elders with deference.

- *A simple gesture of bowing your head* or saying "Khop chai" (forgive me) can resolve differences.

5. Embrace language learning opportunities:

Laos offers a wealth of opportunities to learn the Lao language. Consider taking a Lao language course, enrolling in a conversation exchange program, or simply practicing with locals.

- *Every interaction* is an opportunity to learn and grow.

6. Utilize translation tools and apps:

While learning Lao phrases is encouraged, don't hesitate to use translation tools and apps to bridge communication gaps.

- *These tools can help you navigate menus*, ask for directions, and clarify misunderstandings.

7. Be patient and open-minded:

Language barriers are inevitable, but they don't have to hinder your experiences. Approach communication with patience, humor, and an open mind.

8. Show genuine interest and appreciation:

Locals will appreciate your efforts to communicate in their language, even if imperfect. Showing genuine interest will further enhance your interactions.

9. Don't be afraid to make mistakes:

Mistakes are a natural part of the language learning process. Embrace them as opportunities to learn and grow. Laos people are understanding and will appreciate your attempt.

10. Have fun with the process:

Learning a new language should be an enjoyable experience. Embrace the challenges, laugh at your mistakes, and celebrate your progress. The more you engage with the language, the more comfortable and confident you'll become.

"The soul of Laos resides in the rhythmic dance of its traditions and the melody of its landscapes."

- Karen Blixen

Chapter 11:
Essential Information

This section will provide you with the essential information you need to navigate your Laotian adventure with ease and confidence.

Health and Safety

Prioritize your well-being by ensuring your routine vaccinations are up-to-date.

- *Malaria is present in some regions*, so consult your healthcare provider about preventive measures.

- *It's also advisable* to drink bottled or boiled water to stay hydrated.

Weather Considerations

Laos experiences a tropical climate, with distinct wet and dry seasons.

- *Pack accordingly*, keeping in mind lightweight and breathable clothing, sunscreen, and mosquito repellent for added comfort during your explorations.

Souvenirs and Local Crafts

Capture the essence of Laos by bringing home authentic souvenirs. Explore local markets for traditional textiles, handmade crafts, and intricate jewelry.

- *Bargaining is a cultural norm*, so embrace the experience while securing unique treasures.

Responsible Tourism

Contribute positively to the local environment and communities by practicing responsible tourism.

- *Be mindful of the impact* of your actions on the delicate ecosystems and respect the cultural heritage of the places you visit.

Embark on your Laotian journey armed with these essential insights, allowing you to navigate the unique landscape of this enchanting country with confidence and cultural sensitivity.

Frequently Asked Questions (FAQ)

Q1. How can I get a visa for Laos?

Most travelers can get a visa when they arrive in Laos. Make sure to check the latest requirements and fees before you travel to avoid any surprises at the border.

Q2. What money is used in Laos?

The official money in Laos is the Lao Kip (LAK). While bigger cities may accept major currencies, it's a good idea to exchange money when you arrive for a smoother transaction.

Q3. Are there health precautions I should take?

Make sure your routine shots are up-to-date, and talk to your doctor about malaria prevention, especially if you're going to certain places. Drinking bottled or boiled water is a good idea to stay healthy.

Q4. What ways can I travel in Laos?

Laos has many ways to get around, from tuk-tuks to long-tail boats. Talk about prices for tuk-tuks and taxis beforehand, and think about taking the slow boat on the Mekong River for a calm trip.

Q5. What's the main food in Laos?

Laap is the national food of Laos. Don't miss the chance to taste this flavorful dish along with the special Sticky Rice.

Q6. How should I dress when I go to temples?

When you visit temples, dress modestly, covering your shoulders and knees. Remember to take off your shoes before you go in, something everyone does in Laos.

Q7. When is the best time to visit Laos?

Laos has a tropical climate with different wet and dry times. The dry time, from November to March, is good for travel, with nice weather for exploring.

Q8. What local things should I know about?

Show respect by following local ways, like taking off your shoes before going into homes or certain shops. Be polite and use the traditional "wai" gesture.

Q9. Can I use big credit cards in Laos?

While big credit cards work in bigger cities, it's good to have cash, especially in smaller places. There are ATMs in big towns for extra help.

Q10. How can I help the local place when I travel?

Do responsible travel by thinking about how your actions affect the environment and local people. Respect local culture and help local businesses.

Q11. Do a lot of people in Laos speak English?

English is common in tourist places, but in smaller places, it helps to learn a few basic Lao phrases for better talk with locals.

Q12. What cool things can I get in Laos?

Look in local markets for traditional textiles, handmade things, and special jewelry. Bargaining is normal, so enjoy it while you get special things to bring home.

Your trip in Laos is a mix of finding out about culture and seeing great things in nature.

- *By knowing these questions that people often ask,* you'll move through the amazing views and lively traditions with ease, making strong memories of your time in this interesting country.

The Ideal 7-Days Itinerary Plan

Welcome to a week-long journey through the heart of Laos, where ancient traditions and natural wonders await. This carefully crafted itinerary ensures you experience the best of this enchanting country.

Day 1: Arrival in Vientiane

- *Arrive in Vientiane*, the capital city, and ease into your Laotian adventure.
- *Spend the day exploring Wat Si Saket*, the oldest temple in Vientiane, and stroll along the Mekong River promenade as the sun sets.

Day 2: Discovering Vang Vieng

- *Head to Vang Vieng*, a scenic town surrounded by limestone karst mountains.
- *Explore the Tham Chang Cave* and enjoy the breathtaking views from the Nam Xay Viewpoint.
- *In the evening*, savor a traditional Laotian meal by the Nam Song River.

Day 3: Enchanting Luang Prabang

- *Fly to Luang Prabang*, a UNESCO World Heritage Site.

- *Visit the Royal Palace Museum*, explore the vibrant Night Market, and climb Mount Phousi for panoramic sunset views.

- *End the day with a visit* to the atmospheric Wat Xieng Thong.

Day 4: Kuang Si Falls and Hmong Villages

- *Embark on a day trip* to the stunning Kuang Si Falls.

- *Marvel at the turquoise cascades*, visit the Free the Bears sanctuary, and discover traditional Hmong villages.

- *Immerse yourself* in the local culture and enjoy the serene beauty of the surroundings.

Day 5: Journey to Plain of Jars

- *Travel to Phonsavan*, the gateway to the mysterious Plain of Jars.

- *Explore the archaeological sites* and learn about the historical and cultural significance of these ancient stone jars. Witness a beautiful sunset over the plains.

Day 6: Mystical Pakse

- *Fly to Pakse and explore* the ancient temple of Wat Phou, a UNESCO World Heritage Site.
- *Cruise along the Mekong River* to the serene 4,000 Islands (Si Phan Don) and witness the majestic Khone Phapheng Falls, the largest waterfall in Southeast Asia.

Day 7: Don Det Relaxation

- *On your final day*, unwind on the tranquil island of Don Det.
- *Rent a bicycle to explore the island*, interact with locals, and enjoy the laid-back atmosphere.
- *Witness the rare Irrawaddy dolphins* on a boat trip before bidding farewell to the serene beauty of Laos.

This 7-day itinerary provides a perfect blend of cultural exploration, natural wonders, and local experiences.

Final Thoughts

As you reach the final pages of this guide, you've embarked on a virtual journey through Laos, a land of rich culture, breathtaking landscapes, and warm hospitality.

Here are a few final thoughts for you:

- **Embrace the spirit of Sabai Dee:**

You'll encounter the spirit of Sabai Dee, a philosophy deeply embedded in Laotian life, urging you to slow down, savor the moment, and appreciate the simple joys that surround you.

- **Leave your mark with respect:**

Respect local customs, dress modestly, and treat the environment and its inhabitants with care.

We wish you a safe and enjoyable trip!

Until we meet again,

Dan L. Allbeta

Travel Journal

Travel Budget

Travel Budget

	Transportation	Food	Accommodation
Budget			

	Shopping	Subscription	Entertainment
Budget			

Packing Checklist

Packing Checklist

Documents	Clothes	Toiletries

Gadgets	Contacts	Miscellaneous

Travel Itinerary

Travel Itinerary

Day 1

Place To See		
Transportation	**Activity**	**Time**

Day 2

Place To See		
Transportation	**Activity**	**Time**

Travel Itinerary

Day 3

Place To See		
Transportation	**Activity**	**Time**

Day 4

Place To See		
Transportation	**Activity**	**Time**

Travel Itinerary

Day 5

Place To See		
Transportation	**Activity**	**Time**

Day 6

Place To See		
Transportation	**Activity**	**Time**

Travel Itinerary

Day 7

Place To See		
Transportation	Activity	Time

Day 8

Place To See		
Transportation	Activity	Time

Travel Itinerary

Day 9

Place To See		
Transportation	Activity	Time

Day 10

Place To See		
Transportation	Activity	Time

My Notes

My Note

My Note

My Note

My Note

My Note

My Note

My Note

My Note